CONTENTS

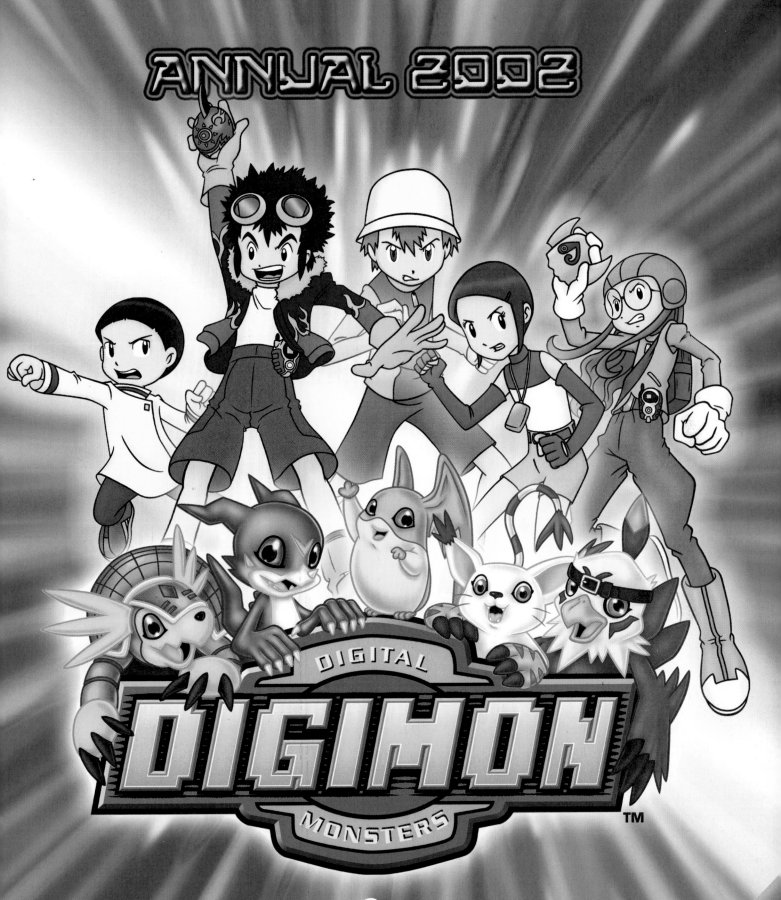

ANNUAL 2002

DIGITAL DIGIMON MONSTERS™

Pedigree®

Published by Pedigree Books Limited.
The Old Rectory, Matford Lane, Exeter EX2 4PS
E-mail: books@pedigreegroup.co.uk
Published 2001

£6.99

DAVIS

A natural ringleader, Davis is full of spunk and prone to losing his temper. But he is very dependable when the going gets tough. Because he is jealous of T.K. and Kari's friendship, Davis sees T.K. as his rival. The goggles Davis wears were once Tai's, whom Davis admires.

CRESTS

FRIENDSHIP COURAGE

KARI

Kari's gentle and unassuming nature has given way to occasional recklessness.
But she also has good judgement and natural leadership skills.
She's the one most likely to lead bad Digimon into traps, and gets excited every time she returns to Digiworld.

CRESTS

LIGHT

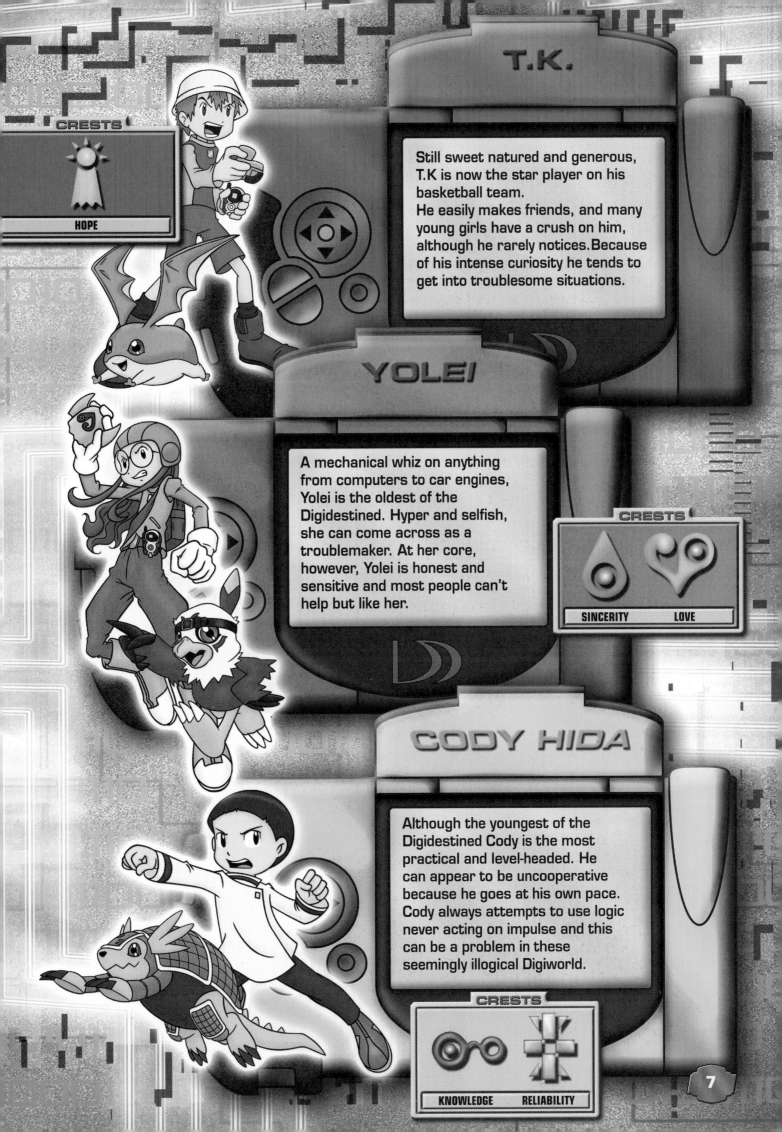

CRESTS

HOPE

T.K.

Still sweet natured and generous, T.K is now the star player on his basketball team.
He easily makes friends, and many young girls have a crush on him, although he rarely notices. Because of his intense curiosity he tends to get into troublesome situations.

YOLEI

A mechanical whiz on anything from computers to car engines, Yolei is the oldest of the Digidestined. Hyper and selfish, she can come across as a troublemaker. At her core, however, Yolei is honest and sensitive and most people can't help but like her.

CRESTS

SINCERITY **LOVE**

CODY HIDA

Although the youngest of the Digidestined Cody is the most practical and level-headed. He can appear to be uncooperative because he goes at his own pace. Cody always attempts to use logic never acting on impulse and this can be a problem in these seemingly illogical Digiworld.

CRESTS

KNOWLEDGE **RELIABILITY**

BABY STAGE

Name: Chikomon
Power:

IN-TRAINING

Name: Demiveemon
Power: Bubble Blow

VEEMON

Veemon is the joker of the Digimon and is always smiling and laughing, however there is a a more serious side to Veemon when it is needed especially when under attack. He has a fierce special power called Vee Head Butt attack, is classified as a Dragon Digimon and his partner is Davis.

ROOKIE

Name: Veemon
Power: Vee Head Butt

ARMOUR EVOLUTION

Name: Flamedramon
Power: Fire Rocket

4 LEGS-ARMOUR EVOLUTION

Name: Raidramon
Power: Blue Thunder

Name: Patamon
Power: Boom Bubble

Name: Angemon
Power: Hand of Fate

Name: Pegasusmon
Power: Shooting Stars

PATAMON

Patamon is a mammal Digimon and is described a bit like a mouse with wings. However despite being very small he protects TK with all his energy, especially by using his special power Boom Bubble. It doesn't sound particularly effective but it has been proved on more than one occasion to be fierce.

GATOMON

At first Gatomon looks a little bit like a kitten but there is definitely a lot of differences, one being the large green paws she has and also the large red claws attached to her paws. She has extremely fast reactions which make her excellent while trying to protect Kari. She is an animal Digimon and her special power is Lightning Claw!!

Name: Nefertimon
Power: Rosetta Stones

Name: Gatomon
Power: Lightning Paw

Name: Angewomon
Power: Celestial Arrow

Name: Poromon
Power: Bubble Blow

IN-TRAINING

Name: Upamon
Power: Bubble Blow

ROOKIE

Name: Dillimon
Power: Claw Chop

ARMOUR EVOLUTION

Name: Digmon
Power: Drill of Power

HAWK
Hawkr
and lo
like a
distinc
very p
you, h
Yolei.
togeth
team a
His sp
Buzzsa
of all t

DILLOMON
Dillomon likes the easy life and always tries to find the simplest way out of a situation. If this does not happen then beware as he has a bit of a temper.

His special power is Claw Chop which combined with his strength makes him an excellent protector and partner to Cody Hida.

4 LEGS-ARMOUR EVOLUTION

Name: Submarimon
Power: Torpedo

Name: Hawkmon
Power: Beak Buzzsaw

Name: Shurimon
Power: Special Stars

Name: Halsemon
Power: Tempest Wing

a Bird Digimon
xactly like he sounds
He also has a very
ccent as he sounds
t don't let this fool
edicated to protecting
they are put
ey make a great
y are both so clever.
ower is Beak
d he is the calmest
gimon.

DIGIMON EMPEROR

A Genius who excels at
sports, the boy named Ken
Ichijoji is self-centered and
egomaniacal. In Digiworld,
he is the ruthless Digimon
Emperor who uses Digimon
as tools to attack and cause
harm. But is he the real
threat to Digiworld, or a
pawn in someone else's
evil scheme?

Name: Minomon

Name: Leafmon

Name: Wormmon

Veemon
Rookie

Have a look at the example, this shows the different stages of a digivolve. Try your own digivolve by first creating your own Digimon and then take it through the rookie, armour evolution and the 4-legs armour evolution stages.

Flamedramon
Armour Evolution

Raidramon
4-Legs Armour Evolution

DIGIVOLVE

Rookie

Armour Evolution

4-Legs Armour Evolution

13

KABUTERIMON'S ELECTRO SHOCKER!

WE'VE PASSED THIS PLACE BEFORE.

YOU MEAN WE WALKED ALL THE WAY AROUND THE WHOLE PLANET?

THAT JUST CAN'T BE. I CAN'T WALK THAT FAR, CAN I? I'M SO TIRED.

MY FEET ARE HOT...

LOOKS LIKE WE'RE TAKIN' A BREAK.

IT'S NOT LIKE WE HAVE SOMEPLACE TO BE.

I GUESS YOU'RE RIGHT. NO REASON TO HURRY.

CHECK OUT IZZY. I BET HE'S TRYING TO E-MAIL THE ALIENS.

STILL CRASHED -- AND THE WARRANTY EXPIRED.

HEY IZZY, I KNOW HOW TO GET IT TO BOOT UP. YA JUST GOTTA GIVE IT A COUPLE OF SUBTLE ADJUSTMENTS.

HEY! ARE YOUR BRAIN CELLS MALFUNCTIONING?!

GEEZ, YOU WOULD THINK I'M HURTIN' THE DUMB THING.

TOO BAD YOUR BRAIN ISN'T AS BIG AS YOUR HAIR MAYBE IZZY DOESN'T WANT GRIMY FINGERPRINTS AND DENTS ALL OVER HIS COMPUTER.

HMMPH.

DO YOU GUYS SEE SMOKE OVER THERE?

I'LL CHECK IT OUT.

HEY, TAI, WAIT FOR ME.

WHATEVER.

WE GOT GRAPHICS, WE GOT SOUND.

BEAUTIFUL! UP AND RUNNING. BUT THE BATTERY NEEDS RECHARGING.

GET OVER HERE, QUICK!

LOOKS LIKE SOME KIND OF FACTORY.

WHAT DO YOU SUPPOSE THEY MAKE IN THERE?

I DON'T KNOW, BUT WOULDN'T IT BE GREAT IF THERE'S A MANUFACTURER'S OUTLET STORE? THEY ALWAYS HAVE KILLER DEALS.

THERE DOESN'T SEEM TO BE ANYBODY HERE.

THERE'S GOTTA BE SOMEONE RUNNING THE EQUIPMENT.

IT APPEARS TO BE DOING QUITE WELL ALL BY ITSELF.

MATT, WHAT ARE THE MACHINES MAKING?

YOU GOT ME. MAYBE PARTS FOR ROBOTS OR SPACE SHIPS.

SOMEBODY'S GOTTA BE MOVIN' THOSE BELTS. AND PEOPLE GOTTA EAT, SO IS THERE A CAFETERIA IN THIS PLACE, 'CUZ WE COULD REALLY USE A GOOD MEAL!

WE CAN COVER MORE GROUND IF WE SPLIT UP...

HELLO?! IS ANYBODY HERE?!

WAIT A MINUTE. DON'T GO ANY FURTHER IN THIS DIRECTION.

WHAT IS IT, BIYOMON?

I'M NOT SURE. I HEARD SOMETHING.

SWOOSH... CRUNCH!

DOESN'T SOUND GOOD TO ME.

ELSEWHERE...

POWER SUPPLY R.

I SAY WE GO INSIDE AND HAVE A LOOK AROUND.

GASP!

DEADLINE

HDR 2000

ISSE

A BATTERY LIKE THAT COULD RUN MY COMPUTER FOREVER... I WONDER IF THERE'S A WAY TO ACCESS ITS POWER.

MEANWHILE...

HEY!

WHAT DO YOU SUPPOSE HAPPENED TO HIM?

WHO KNOWS, BUT LET'S SEE IF WE CAN HELP.

IT'S JUST A BUSTED ROBOT.

IT'S NOT A ROBOT. IT'S ANDROMON.

WHAT? THIS BIG KLUNK IS A DIGIMON?

YEAH, AND VERY ADVANCED.

POOR THING. I GUESS HE GOT CAUGHT IN THE GEARS AND GOT MANGLED.

MAYBE IF WE WORK TOGETHER, WE CAN PULL HIM OUTTA THERE.

MY MOM REALLY DOESN'T WANT ME MOVING ANY HEAVY OBJECTS. I'VE GOT BAD KNEES.

RELAX. WE'LL DO IT.

RIGHT!

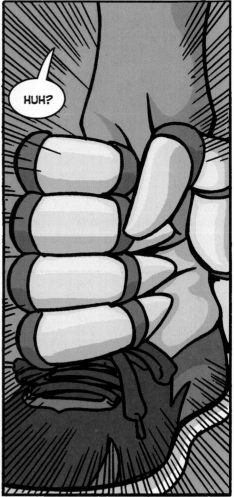

20

FORGET WHAT I SAID ABOUT HIM BEING FRIENDLY!

I SHALL PUNISH ALIEN INTRUDERS.

LET'S GIVE HIM WHAT WE GOT!

SPIRAL TWISTER!

RAAAAGH!

UHG!

AGUMON, HOW ABOUT TRYING TO BLAST THE ROOF?

EEEEYAH!

SKREEE...

CRASH

UHHHH!

BOY, HE'S GONNA HAVE ONE UGLY HEADACHE.

NO DOUBT.

NOW, LET'S GET OUT OF HERE!

MEANWHILE...

WHAT YA DOIN', IZZY?

I'M TRYING TO TAP INTO THIS POWER SOURCE.

IF I CAN GET THIS BABY TO FIRE UP, WE CAN USE MY COMPUTER TO GET HELP.

AH-HA! I'VE LOCATED AN ACCESS PANEL TO THE INTERIOR OPERATIONS.

HEY, LET ME SEE, IZZY. WHAT EXACTLY DO YOU THINK THIS IS?

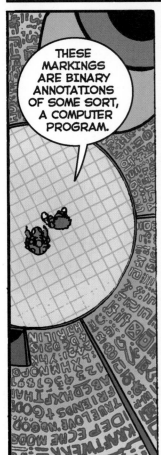

THESE MARKINGS ARE BINARY ANNOTATIONS OF SOME SORT, A COMPUTER PROGRAM.

A VERY COMPLICATED PROGRAM, INDEED.

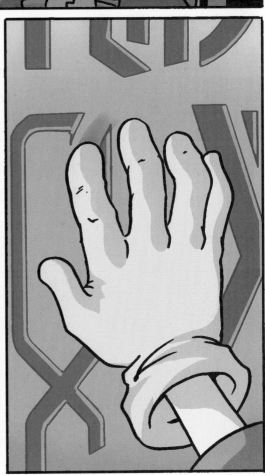

23

BACK AT THE POWER ROOM...

COULD I HAVE DELETED THE WRONG PROGRAM?

I THINK THAT THAT'S A DISTINCT POSSIBILITY. WHY DON'T YOU TRY TO UN-DELETE IT?

GOOD IDEA.

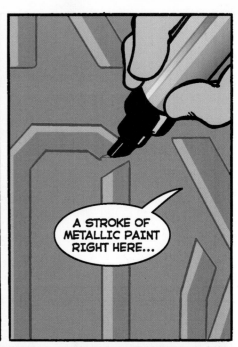

A STROKE OF METALLIC PAINT RIGHT HERE...

I ADMIRE THE WAY YOU KEEP WORKING WHILE YOUR FRIENDS ARE OUT HAVING FUN. DON'T YOU EVER FEEL SORT OF LEFT OUT?

NOT AT ALL. I'M JUST TRYING TO DETERMINE HOW WE ALL GOT TO THIS PLACE.

AND I'D LIKE TO LEARN MORE ABOUT YOU DIGIMON, PERHAPS PROVE SOME OF MY THEORIES.

```
102   /*   fwsc sample... coast creation*/
110   float   s
120   while  s  (1 or s)=2
132   input  "ration 1 to 2 "; s
142   endwhile
152   k=  screen (e and i) = 4th
162   end
172   kw3 = screen fractional
182   rod/ rod1/ rod3/   float
192   r= read () * read () * read (D)
200   input "ration 1 or  s ) = 2
230   screen 1.3.4.5.
240   endd
```

THEORIES, THEORIES. WHAT'S THE BIG MYSTERY? I AM WHO I AM.

REALLY?

I SIMPLY CAN'T UNDERSTAND THIS PREOCCUPATION WITH WHO YOU ARE.

IS THERE SOME KIND OF DEEP DARK SECRET IN YOUR ORIGINS?

OH, WELL...

DON'T YOU THINK IT'S TIME WE TOLD IZZY THE TRUTH, DEAR?

NO. I'M AFRAID IF WE TOLD HIM NOW IT MIGHT BE TOO BIG A SHOCK.

I KNOW YOU'RE TRYING TO DO WHAT'S BEST, BUT I WORRY, ONCE HE FINDS OUT, HE'LL BE UPSET THAT WE DIDN'T TELL HIM SOONER.

HONEY, WE JUST CAN'T THINK ABOUT THAT NOW...

IZZY?! IZZY?!

HUH?! UH, WHAT DID YA SAY?

YOU WERE OFF IN ANOTHER WORLD.

I'M STARTING TO FEEL STRANGE...

TENTOMON TO IZZY -- ARE YOU READING ME?

THIS IS MERELY SPECULATION, BUT I BELIEVE I'VE STUMBLED ON TO SOMETHING MORE THAN JUST A COMPUTER GAME.

OH MY, IT'S GETTING HOT IN HERE. OW! OW! I'M BURNING UP. DO SOMETHING, QUICKLY! I'M BEING ZAPPED!

WHAT'S GOING ON? HEY!

OOH! OUCH! I CAN'T STAND IT! HELP!

HMM, IS IT SHORT-CIRCUITING?

OOH! EEE! MERCY! YIKES!

I'M DISCONNECTING THE POWER. NOW I MAY NEVER FIGURE THE MYSTERY OUT.

WHOOOOO...

WHAT HAPPENED TO MY DIGIVICE?

MEANWHILE, ON THE ROOF...

I KNOW THIS DOESN'T MAKE ANY SENSE, BUT THIS ENTIRE FACTORY IS DESIGNED TO PUT THINGS TOGETHER AND THEN TAKE THEM APART.

I REALLY, REALLY HOPE THEY DESIGNED IT WITH A DOOR!

WHO KNOWS!

IT'S BASED ON PERPETUAL MOTION. NOTHING EVER STOPS, OR LEAVES.

HEY, EVERYBODY! YOU'LL NEVER GUESS WHAT I JUST DISCOVERED?

WHAT'S UP?

WELL, THE COMPUTER PROGRAM OPERATING THIS FACTORY IS PRODUCING THE POWER TO KEEP IT GOING.

EVEN MORE INCREDIBLE, IN DIGIWORLD, BASIC DATA IS A LIVING, VIABLE SUBSTANCE. IT'S ALIVE...

HEY, GUYS! LISTEN UP!

WE GOTTA GET OUT OF HERE. NOW!

WHAT DO YOU MEAN, TAI?

CAPTURE INTRUDERS! SENSORS DETECT HOSTILITY.

BRING INTRUDERS INTO FIRING RANGE.

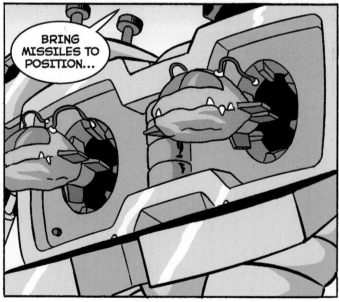

BRING MISSILES TO POSITION...

...AND FIRE!

HELP, MATT!

T.K.!

LOOK OUT!

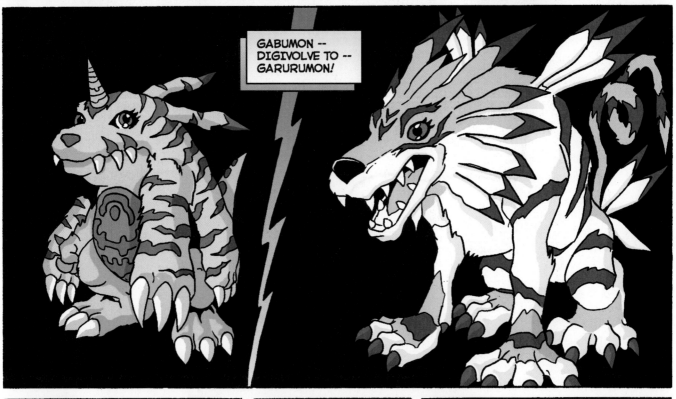

GABUMON -- DIGIVOLVE TO -- GARURUMON!

OH, NO!

BA-BOOM!

BAM-BAM-BAM-BAM-BAM!

AGUMON -- DIGIVOLVE TO -- GREYMON!

SWOOSH!

BOOM!

WHO CHALLENGES ANDROMON?

BUNGLING WEAKLINGS!

YOU PUNY ONES DARE TO CHALLENGE ME?

HE'S MORE POWERFUL THAN EITHER OF OUR DIGIMON!

MAYBE BECAUSE HE'S ALL MACHINE. IT'S ALMOST LIKE HE'S DIGIVOLVED FAR BEYOND THE OTHER DIGIMON.

IS IT POSSIBLE WE COULD LOSE?

SMASH!

TRY RE-ENTERING THAT PROGRAM THAT ACTIVATED YOUR DIGIVICE.

I BELIEVE THAT'S THE KEY TO MY DIGIVOLVING.

YES!

IT'S GOT TO WORK...

IF I CAN JUST RECALL THE EXACT SEQUENCE...

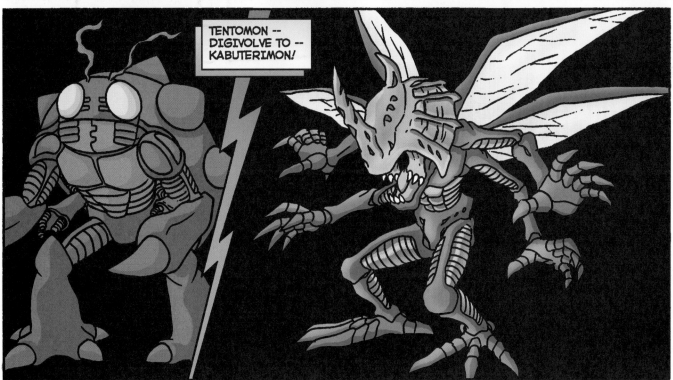

TENTOMON -- DIGIVOLVE TO -- KABUTERIMON!

RAAAAAAH!

GRRAAAAAH!!!

DOESN'T THAT ANDROMON EVER RUN OUTTA GAS?

THAT'S IT... CUT HIS POWER!

DEMOBILIZE HIS RIGHT LEG, AND WE'LL INTERRUPT HIS ENERGY SOURCE.

ZZT!

ELECTRO SHOCKER!

ZZT! ZZT!

HE STRIPPED A GEAR!

THAT'S WICKED!

MOMENTS LATER...

THAT BLACK GEAR REPROGRAMMED MY SYSTEM SOMEHOW. I'M NORMALLY A NONVIOLENT DIGIMON.

YOU COULDA FOOLED US!

I NEVER MEANT TO HURT ANYONE.

PERHAPS I CAN BE OF SOME HELP. THE BEST WAY TO ESCAPE FROM HERE IS TO FOLLOW THE UNDERGROUND WATERWAY...

THE LABYRINTH BEGINS JUST BEYOND THIS POINT.

THANKS FOR YOUR HELP, ANDROMON.

I HOPE YOU FIND YOUR WAY HOME AND, NO MATTER WHAT, TRY TO REMEMBER THE BIG GUY THAT TURNED OUT TO BE NOT SO BAD.

THERE'S ONE THING YOU CAN COUNT ON-- WE'LL NEVER FORGET YOU, ANDROMON!

DIGIMAZE

TK and Patamon are lost in the factory. Help them find their way out to the underground tunnels. Start at the Assembly Plant. On the way they must pass through the Power Room and over the factory Roof.

ASSEMBLY PLANT

POWER ROOM

FACTORY ROOF

UNDERGROUND TUNNELS

DIGIWORD

Try to fill in the crossword above by answering the questions below, they are based on Digimon general knowledge and the story "Togemon in Toy Town".

1. Gatomon is who's Digimon?
2. One of the kids has a second name HIDA what is his first name?
3. What special power does Palmon use against Monzaemon?
4. What is name of Davis' Rookie Digimon?
5. Which kid in the story does Mimi comment "does not talk like that" ?
6. Which kid does Hawkmon belong to?
7. Who gets upset and starts crying at the beginning of the story?
9. Palmon digivolves into which Digimon?
9. What is the name of the town that the kids visit in the story?
8. In the story what is the name of Mimi's Digimon?
10. Veemon digivolves into which Digimon?
11. What is the name of Yolei's In Training Digimon?
12. In the story which Digimon wrote the song?

DIGICODE

ABCDEFGHIJKLMNOPQRSTUVWXYZ

The power source from the factory has a Binary Annotation on the inside this creates the a special code, help Izzy break the code by unscrambling the short messages below as practice. The messages are all typical phrases used within Digiworld. Good luck!!

BREAKER

Now try to decode these
questions and answer them .
Answers are on page 108.

1. ⟨decoded question text⟩

2. ⟨decoded question text⟩

3. ⟨decoded question text⟩

4. ⟨decoded question text⟩

5. ⟨decoded question text⟩

6. ⟨decoded question text⟩

7. ⟨decoded question text⟩

OF ALL THE STRANGE THINGS THAT HAPPENED TO US ON DIGIMON ISLAND, I NEVER EXPECTED TO FIND A SECRET ADMIRER IN THE SEWER...

OKAY, EVERYBODY, LET'S SING THE SONG THAT AGUMON WROTE!

DIGIMON EAT, THEN DIGIMON FIGHT-- DIGIMON DIGIVOLVE AND FIGHT ALL NIGHT!

DIGIMON FIGHT AND DIGIMON FLY-- DIGIMON DIGI--

AAH!!

AWWWW...

>SOB<

SORA, ARE YOU ALRIGHT?

38

YEAH, WHAT'S THE MATTER?

WATER FELL FROM UP THERE ...

THAT MADE YOU SCREAM?

YEAH...NO ... UH...I USED TO SING AT HOME. I USED TO SING TO MYSELF ALL THE TIME WHILE I WAS DOING MY CHORES.

"WHEN I'D HANG CLOTHES TO DRY OUTSIDE I'D SING REALLY LOUD 'CAUSE NOBODY COULD HEAR ME THERE."

IT'S OKAY TO MISS YOUR HOME, SORA.

"I MISS PLAYING SPORTS, THEN TAKING A NICE HOT BATH."

I MISS GOING ON VACATIONS!

39

"NOTHING BEATS HAVING A COOL DRINK ON A SUMMER'S DAY AT THE BEACH! I LOVE THE OCEAN AIR!"

THEY REALLY DO COME FROM ANOTHER WORLD...

THAT IS WHY THEY ARE DEPRESSED.

QUIET! LISTEN, EVERYONE--!

GOBBLE slurp

NUMEMON!

REALLY DISGUSTING DIGIMON WHO LIVE DOWN HERE IN THE SEWERS.

GOBBLE GOBBLE blah

THERE'S SO MANY OF THEM--!

--HURRY! RUN!

slurp GOBBLE burp

THEY LOOK SO SMALL. WHY ARE WE RUNNING?!

YOU'LL SEE--KEEP RUNNING!

THESE NEW SEWER-DWELLING DIGIMON WERE LIKE TOTALLY HYGIENE DEFICIENT!

gah GOBBLE

LET 'EM HAVE IT!

THEY LOVED THROWING "NUMESLUDGE" AT YOU ... AND THEY HAD BAD BREATH, TOO!

THIS-A-WAY!

GOBBLE gob

OOOH!

41

THANK GOODNESS WE FINALLY ESCAPED THOSE NUMEMONS, ONCE WE GOT OUTSIDE. WE DIDN'T SEE ANYTHING ELSE FOR MILES, UNTIL WE SAW THE STRANGEST THING ...

I BET THERE'S ENOUGH SNACKS TO LAST US A LIFETIME! AT LEAST!

MIMI, THEY PROBABLY DON'T WORK. DON'T YOU REMEMBER THE PHONE BOOTHS?

*DIGIMON ISSUE 2!

EVEN IF THEY'RE REAL, YOU KNOW THEY'RE NOT PLUGGED IN!

I WON'T ACCEPT THAT!

MIMI!

YOU CAN'T STOP HER. SHE'S SO STUBBORN.

YEA! SODA! YOU WANT ONE?

NO, I DON'T!

YOU DON'T HAVE TO BITE MY HEAD OFF!

43

THIS IS IT, MIMI. TOY TOWN!

WOW, IT REALLY LOOKS BEAUTIFUL! KINDA LIKE A BIG AMUSEMENT PARK--!

IT DOESN'T LOOK LIKE ANYONE'S HERE.

SOMETHING'S NOT RIGHT, MIMI.

OH BOY, THIS IS FUN!

THIS IS REALLY FUN!

TAI?!

BOY, I'M REALLY HAVING A LOT OF FUN NOW!

THAT DOESN'T LOOK LIKE A LOT OF FUN.

THIS IS SO EXCITING! THIS IS REALLY EXCITING!

JUST WHAT'S GOING ON HERE?!

47

49

HEARTS ATTACK, THOSE TWO!

YOU'LL SEE, TOY TOWN IS THE GREATEST PLACE TO BE!

YOU'RE ALL GOING INTO OUR NEW COMMUNITY TOY BOX!

OUR TOY BOX IS ONLY FILLED WITH CHILDREN!

SO THE TOYS HAVE BEEN PLAYING WITH THEM!

AGU, TELL US, WHAT CHANGED MONZAEMON?

WE DON'T KNOW.

IT'S UP TO YOU TWO! YOU MUST BE THE HEROES THIS TIME.

WHAT DO YOU MEAN?

YOU MUST DEFEAT MONZAEMON!

YOU'RE KIDDING!

WE CAN'T GET FREE! YOU HAVE TO SAVE THE OTHERS!

MONAZEMON'S HEARTS AREN'T SUPPOSED TO ATTACK, ONLY GIVE "HEART HUGS," WHICH GIVE PEOPLE SUCH A GOOD FEELING THAT IT MAKES THEM WANT TO HELP OTHERS--

IT'S SUCH A HAPPY DAY IN TOY TOWN!

MONZAEMON!

YOU'LL LIKE THESE! EVERYONE LIKES THE BALLOONS!

HEY, YETI-TEDDY! WHATEVER YOU'VE DONE TO MY FRIENDS, FIX IT NOW, OR YOU'LL BE IN TROUBLE! YA UNDERSTAND ME?!

THIS ISN'T FUNNY! I'M BEING CHASED BY A GIANT STUFFED BEAR!

I'LL SAVE YA, HONEY!

GRRRRR

NUMEMON!

YOU TURN HIM DOWN, HE STILL HELPS?!

WELL, PALMON, WHAT CAN I SAY-- WHEN YOU'VE GOT IT, YOU'VE GOT IT!

OH NO, THE NUMESLUDGE ISN'T WORKING!

I CAN'T LET THEM FIGHT ALONE!

POISON IVY!

PALMON, BE CAREFUL!

53

blah aah! GOBBLE

NUMEMON!

I MAY BE A LADY, BUT I AM NOT A PUSHOVER!

PALMON DIGIVOLVE TO--

--TOGEMON!

YOU'RE GOING DOWN, BIG BOY!

GRRRRRR!!

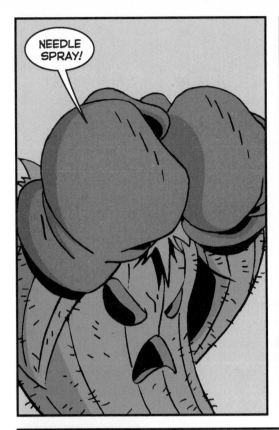

NEEDLE SPRAY!

GRRRRRR!!

RAAHH

PALMON!

YOU'RE FABULOUS!

MY STEM IS BRUISED!

AFTER EVERYONE WAS FREE FROM THE SPELL, AND THE TRUNK, MONZAEMON TOLD US WHAT REALLY HAPPENED ...

USUALLY, WHEN KIDS GET TIRED OF THEIR TOYS, THEY JUST ABANDON THEM. THEY THROW THEM AWAY. SO I CREATED A HOME FOR THOSE TOYS.

I WANTED TO MAKE THE TOYS MORE IMPORTANT TO THEIR OWNERS, AND I FOUND A WAY TO LET THEIR OWNERS WALK IN THEIR SHOES...

HOW, BY TURNING KIDS INTO ZOMBIES?

I DIDN'T MEAN FOR THAT TO HAPPEN. I REALLY AM SORRY ABOUT IT. BUT AN EVIL FEELING CAME OVER ME...

IT HAD TO BE THAT BLACK GEAR!

YOU KNOW, I'M BEGINNING TO TAKE THIS WHOLE BLACK GEAR THING A LITTLE PERSONALLY. THEY CAUSE A WHOLE LOT OF TROUBLE BEFORE DISAPPEARING.

THAT'S RIGHT, BUT ME AND PALMON MADE MONZAEMON GOOD AGAIN!

WE'RE A GREAT TEAM!

MY FRIENDS, THERE'S ONLY ONE WAY THAT I CAN TRULY SHOW MY GRATITUDE, AND THAT'S BY GIVING ALL OF YOU A REAL HEART HUG!

PICTURE

Look at the picture below of the Digimon and see if you can copy the picture by using the grid underneath it, then colour it in.

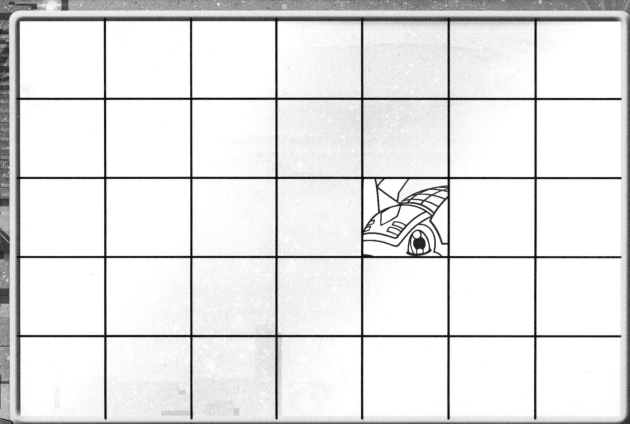

PERFECT

How well do you know your Digimon characters? Look at the pictures, and see if you can fill in the crossword below!

DIGI RINGS

The picture below has a number Dark Rings hidden inside it. Can you find how many of them there are before they get to the Digimon?

POWER MATCH

The Digimon have special powers that they use to protect themselves. Can you match the Digimon to it's special power and colour it in?

LIGHTNING PAW

SHOOTING STARS

BEAK BUZZSAW

CLAW CHOP

VEE HEAD BUTT

Can you recognise
these Digimon?
They are in disguise
to escape the Evil
Digimon Emperor.

A

B

C

D

E

F

G

H

FUN WITH FACES

These Characters only have half of their faces. Do you know your Digimon well enough to draw the other half and colour it in?

HEY, LOOK OVER *THERE!*

WONDER WHAT IT IS.

I KNOW! IT'S A BIG! GEYSER!

SOON...

YEAH! *NOW* I CAN TAKE A *BATH!*

AND WE CAN GET WARM!

UH-OH, THIS WATER'S *WAAAY* TOO *HOT!*

WE'D BE *COOKED* IF WE JUMPED IN.

YES, TENTOMON, WE'D BE *BOILED.*

SUNNY-SIDE UP EGGS ARE MY SPECIALTY!

SORA, THESE ARE *GREAT!* I HAVEN'T HAD A MEAL LIKE THIS IN A LONG TIME.

WHATSA MATTER, JOE? YOU HAVEN'T EATEN ANYTHING.

JOIN THE FUN, JOE!

IT'S TOO LATE FOR HIM.

70

I HAVE TO *THINK* OF SOMETHING... AND *FAST!*

IF I'M RESPONSIBLE FOR EVERYONE'S SAFETY, THEN I HAVE TO P*ROTECT* THEM.

THEIR LIVES DEPEND ON *ME.*

I'VE ALWAYS BEEN *GOOD* AT *CLIMBING.*

I'VE GOT THE *BEST* CHANCE OF MAKING IT TO THE TOP.

NOT GONNA CLIMB THAT MOUNTAIN BY *YOURSELF*, ARE YA?

GOMAMON?!

YUP! FORGOT ME *ALREADY*?

WHY DON'T YOU JUST GO BACK TO SLEEP?!

I DON'T THINK SO.

YOU'RE NOT GOING, SO STOP *FOLLOWING*!

I'M *NOT* FOLLOWING.

I HAVE BUSINESS OF MY OWN TO TAKE CARE OF UP THERE. EVERYTHING DOESN'T *REVOLVE* AROUND *YOU*, Y'KNOW!

FINE! FINE!

SOMETIMES, YOU JUST HAVE TO TRICK 'EM.

WHAT?

NOTHING, JOE.

SOON...

INFINITY MOUNTAIN IS MUCH *BIGGER* THAN I THOUGHT IT WAS!

WE CAN TURN AROUND. ARE YOU READY TO *QUIT?*

OF COURSE NOT!

GOTCHA!

A LITTLE HELP!

CAN'T... STOP... NOW...

IT LOOKS TO ME LIKE WE'RE HALFWAY THERE.

WE MAKE QUITE A *TEAM!*

ACTUALLY, WE *DO!* YOU'RE RIGHT!

WHAT'S TH-*THAT?!* DO YOU THINK THE M-MOUNTAIN IS A V-V-*VOLCANO?*

78

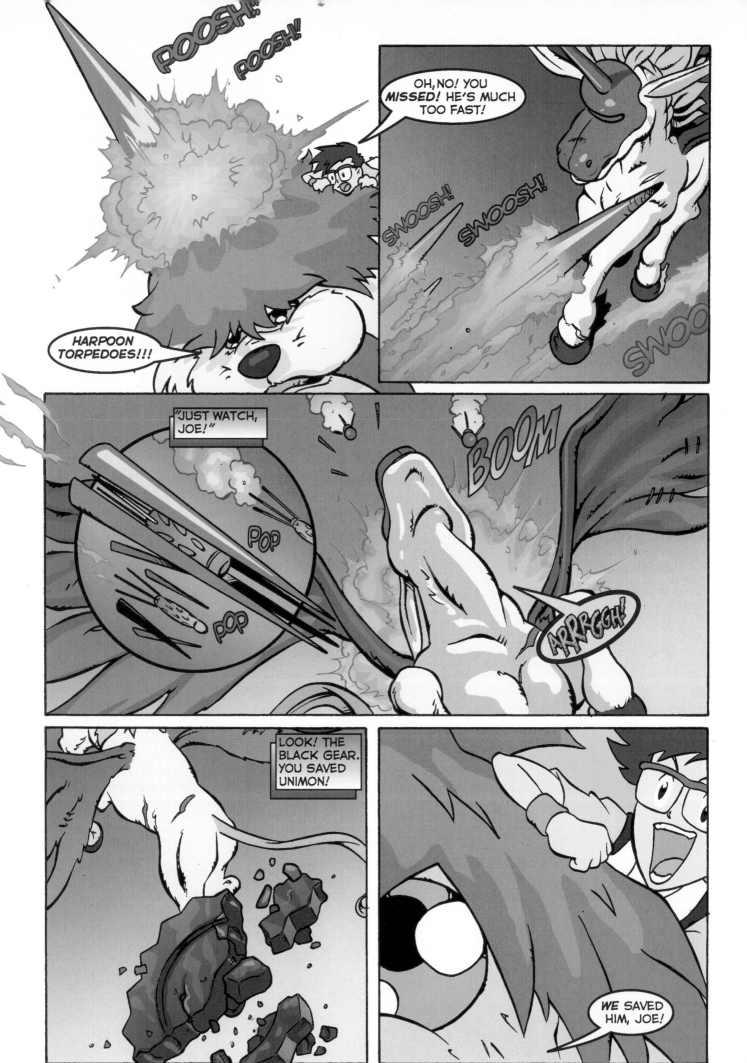

EGGSTRA FUN

 Courage — **8** Points

 Friendship — **7** Points

 Hope — **6** Points

 Light — **5** Points

 Sincerity — **4** Points

 Love — **3** Points

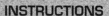 Knowledge — **2** Points

 Reliability — **1** Point

The Digi Eggs that the Digi Destined carry with them are essential to the Digimon to allow them to Digivolve. This game allows you to get to know the Digi Eggs and also have a bit of fun aswell.

INSTRUCTIONS

1. To Start the game place your Digimon Annual on to a flat surface,

2. Then place a 5p coin on the circle at the bottom of the page.

3. Next flick/shove the coin as far up the page as possible so that it lands on one of the points section. The idea of the game is to get as many points as you can, so the further the coin goes the higher the points get!

4. At the end of 10 turns add up your points and the winner is the one with the most.

HAVE FUN!!

DIGIDIFFERENCE

Which of these Digimon is the odd one out and why?

A

B

C

D

E

F

Which of these DigiDestined is the odd one out and why?

G

H

DIGICOLOUR

Colour the Hawkmon and Dillomon to match the ones shown.

DIGIDOT TO DIGIDOT

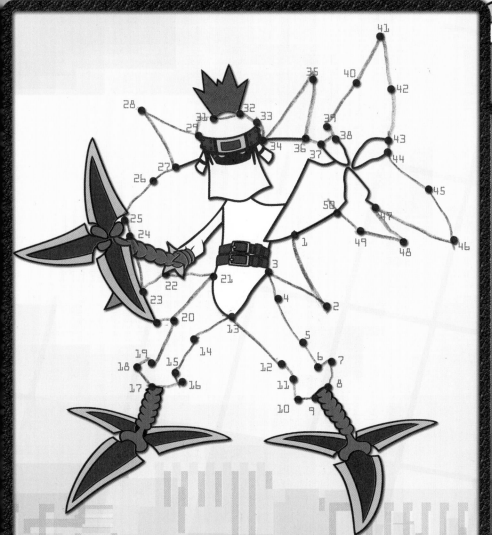

Help these three Digimon. The evil Digimon Emperor has made some of the Digimon invisible, but he has left dots around the outside.

Join the dots by following the numbers to find out which Digimon we cannot see.

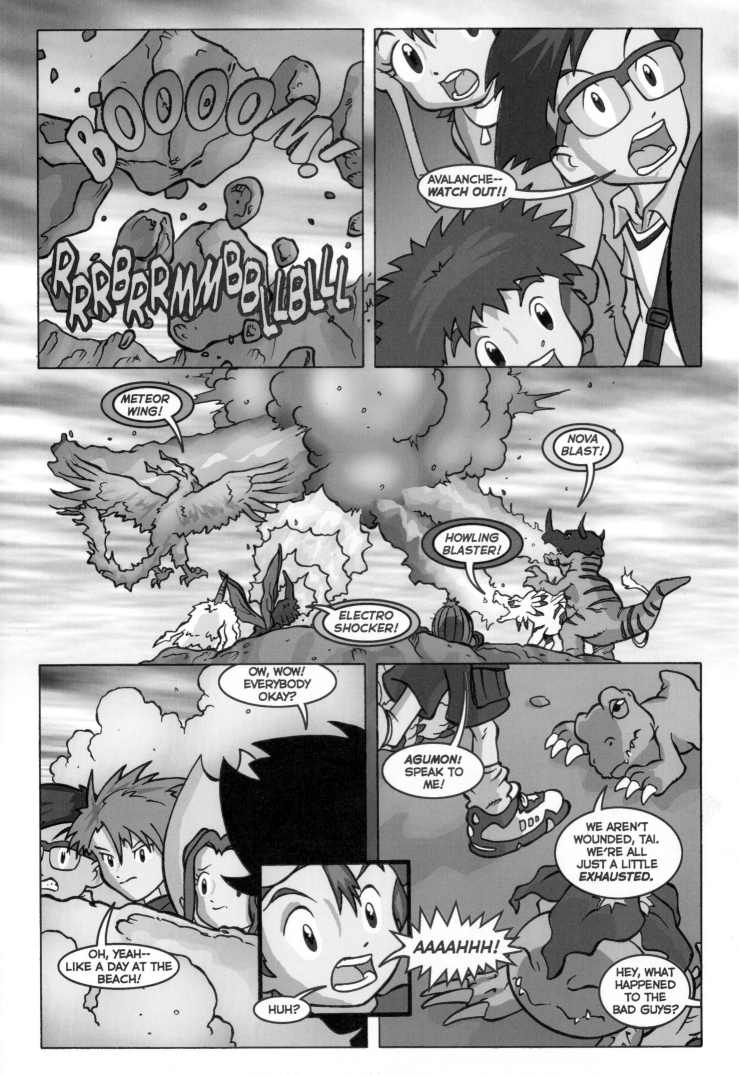

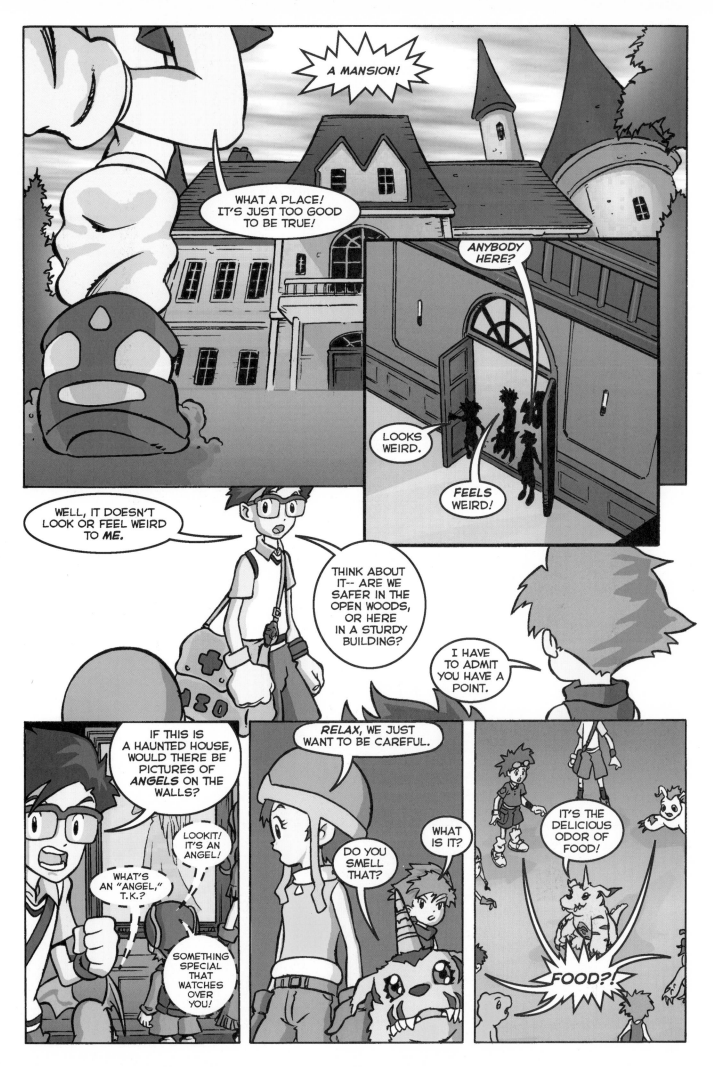

A MANSION!

WHAT A PLACE! IT'S JUST TOO GOOD TO BE TRUE!

ANYBODY HERE?

LOOKS WEIRD.

FEELS WEIRD!

WELL, IT DOESN'T LOOK OR FEEL WEIRD TO ME.

THINK ABOUT IT-- ARE WE SAFER IN THE OPEN WOODS, OR HERE IN A STURDY BUILDING?

I HAVE TO ADMIT YOU HAVE A POINT.

IF THIS IS A HAUNTED HOUSE, WOULD THERE BE PICTURES OF ANGELS ON THE WALLS?

LOOKIT! IT'S AN ANGEL!

WHAT'S AN "ANGEL," T.K.?

SOMETHING SPECIAL THAT WATCHES OVER YOU!

RELAX, WE JUST WANT TO BE CAREFUL.

DO YOU SMELL THAT?

WHAT IS IT?

IT'S THE DELICIOUS ODOR OF FOOD!

FOOD?!

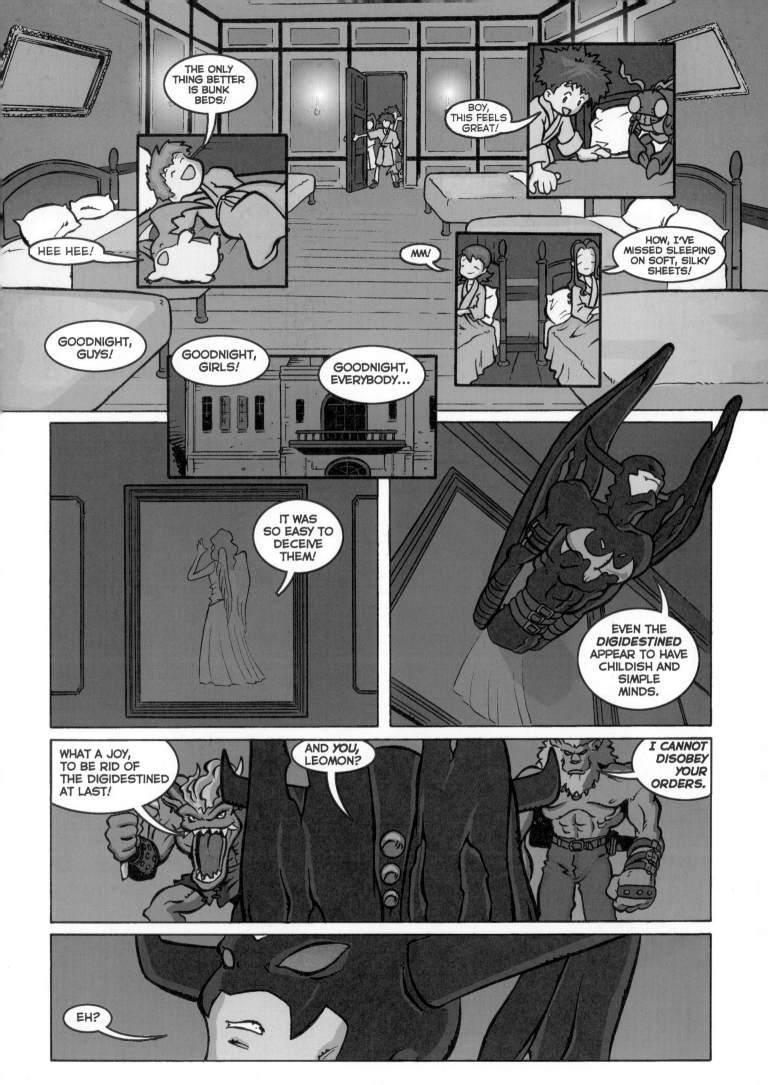

WHHIIOOSSSHHHHHH

I HAVE NO FURTHER USE FOR THIS IMAGINARY BUILDING!

WAAAHH!

WHHOOOOSSSSHHHHX

WAKE UP, EVERYBODY! SOMETHING'S WRONG!

EEEEKK!

WHAT HAPPENED?!

AAAHH!

HELLLLP!

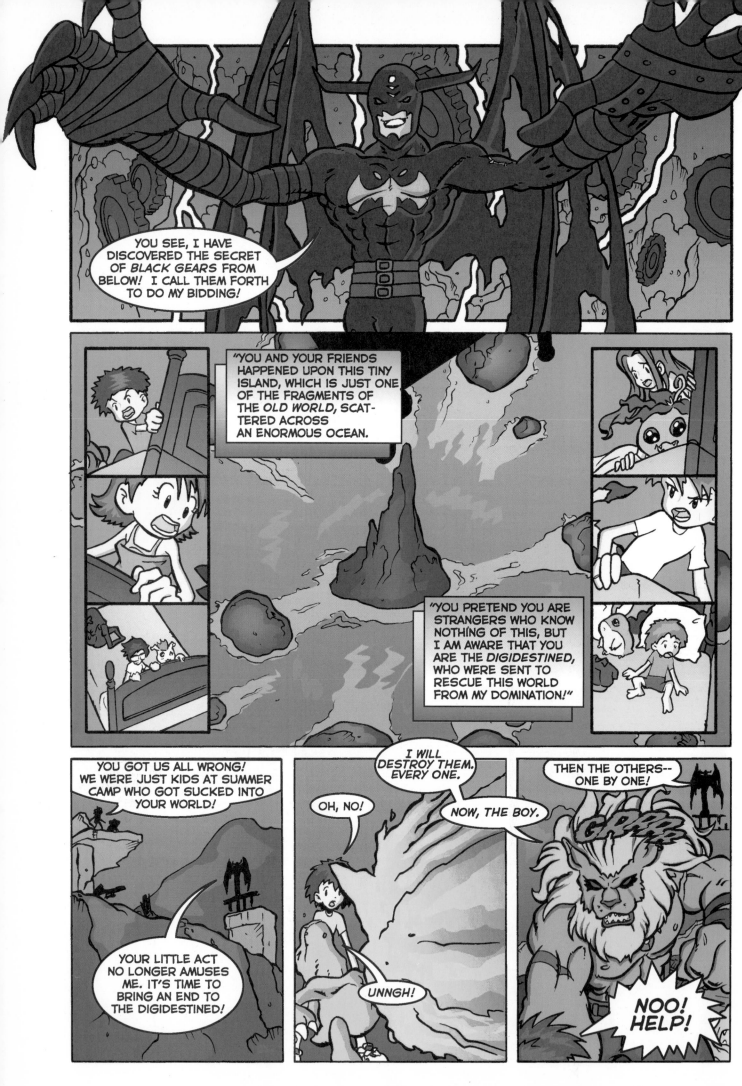

DIGIWORDS

```
K Z D L E F T P G I V X S Z X
C O G A E D M E W D M E I Q P
M B L L X U G P G C Q X Z D F
A M L D I Q X P A R O W Q Z P
P H O A X C R E G X Q I E V J
M X D R C W P R C H F H Q L V
A D I V T K B B S H S H A E S
R V G S E O G R N I M A V O I
O X I F E T Y E F O O D A M V
I K V T W Z D A A H N U L O H
G B O X D J Z T V R H S A N S
X U L A B T L H S X R Q N H V
D E V I M O N H A F Z M C M A
H Q E C K O G R E M O N H E Y
F L D C U M A N S I O N E D P
```

Find these words
LEOMON
OGREMON
DEVIMON
MANSION
FOOD
MAP
BLACK GEAR
PEPPER BREATH
DIGIVOLVED
AVALANCHE

Find these words
DIGIVOLVE
DARKRING
PATAMON
PEGASUSMON
GATOMON
NEFERTIMON
VEEMON
RAIDRAMON
HAWKMON
HALSEMON
DILLOMON

```
P R D I Y S W F D S D U H C P
H W I L R W E X D N R R B R N
P E G A S U S M O N T A E U V
Q P I R P A T A M O N I Y V C
P Y V U W W J Y V P T D K O H
G O O H H X S G A E F R E S A
S S L U C K G C A K E A X D W
F A V D A R K R I N G M K X K
Y I E H A L S E M O N O O B M
S C U A M J U T Z M Y N C N O
L H C B Z N E F E R T I M O N
G A T O M O N F G V G N T Y H
M I D I L L O M O N P N W I O
```

DIGIQUIZ

1. What crest do we associate with TK?
2. What does Angemon digivolve into?
3. What is the special power of Kari's Digimon Gatomon?
4. What is the name of Davis' In Training Digimon?

5. Yolei has two crests what are they?
6. What item do the kids use to Digivolve?
7. Who is Ken Ichijoji better known as?
8. What is Upamons special power?

9. Who does the crest of Courage belong to? —Davis
10. How many stages of digivolution are there for Veemon?
11. Who is the star player of his basketball team?
12. One of the kids wears a pair of goggles that were once Tai's, who is it?

13. Who is the youngest of the Digidestined?
14. What is the name of Kari's Rookie digimon?
15. What is name of Cody Hida's armour evolution Digimon?
16. Which Digimon has a special power called Beak Buzzsaw?

ANSWERS

Page 34 "Digimaze"

Page 35 "Digiword"

1. KARI
2. CODY
3. POISON IVY
4. VEEMON
5. IZZY
6. YOLEI
7. SORA
8. PALMON
9. (Down) TOGEMON
9. (Across) TOY
10. FLAMEDRAMON
11. POROMON

Page 36/37 "Digicode Breaker"

"DIGIVICE POWER"
"DIGIVOLVE IT"
"NEXT STOP, DIGIWORLD"
"DIGIVOLVE IT"

1. TAI
2. A FACTORY
3. ANDROMON
4. BATTERY
5. LIGHTNING BLADE
6. LIGHTS
7. ON THE ROOF

Page 59 "Picture Perfect"

1. DOWN - HALESMON
2. ACROSS - DAVIS
3. DOWN - VEEMON
4. ACROSS - NEFERTIMON
5. ACROSS - PATAMON
6. DOWN - GATOMON
7. DOWN - POROMON
8. ACROSS - FLAMEDRAMON

Page 60 "Digirings"

There are 15 Rings

Page 61 "Power Match"

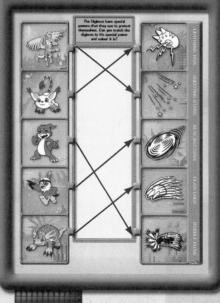

Page 108 "Digiwords"

Page 109 "Digiquiz"

1. CREST OF HOPE
2. PEGASUSMON
3. LIGHTNING PAW
4. DEMIVEEMON
5. SINCERITY & LOVE
6. DIGI EGGS
7. DIGIMON EMPEROR
8. BUBBLE BLOW
9. DAVIS
10. 5
11. TK
12. DAVIS
13. CODY HIDA
14. GATOMON
15. DIGMON
16. HAWKMON

Page 85 "Digidifference"

C - Dillomon is not an Armour Evolution but a Rookie.

H- The Digimon Emperor is Evil.

Page 62 "Fun with Faces"

A - PEGASUSMON
B - GATOMON
C - HAWKMON
D - POROMON
E - VEEMON
F - FLAMEDRAMON
H - HALSEMON
G - DILLOMON